THE NEWNESS
OF
THE NEW COVENANT

A. Blake White

5317 Wye Creek Dr, Frederick, MD 21703-6938
Website: newcovenantmedia.com
Email: info@newcovenantmedia.com
Phone: 301-473-8781 or 800-376-4146
Fax: 240-206-0373

The Newness of the New Covenant

Copyright 2008© by A. Blake White

Published by: New Covenant Media
                  5317 Wye Creek Drive
                  Frederick, Maryland 21703-6938

Orders: www.newcovenantmedia.com

Printed in the United States of America

ISBN 13: 978-1-928965-27-5

TABLE OF CONTENTS

PREFACE

How one puts the canon together is extremely important. Entire denominations are formed based on differing views of how the Old Testament relates to the New. The two most common theological systems dealing with the relationship of the testaments are Dispensationalism and Covenant Theology, but there have been many revisions of each in the last fifty years.[1] Classic Dispensationalism has largely fallen off the map, thanks in large part to the work of George Eldon Ladd (who built off of the insights of Geerhardus Vos and others), while Progressive Dispensationalism and Covenant Theology are still thriving in their various circles. This book will come from a New Covenant Theological perspective. By a brief look at the progressive covenantal framework of the Old Testament, and a closer look at several key texts in the Gospels, Paul, and Hebrews, this book will seek to show that the new covenant is fundamentally and radically *new*.

---

[1] See the collection of essays in John S. Feinberg, ed., *Continuity and Discontinuity: Perspectives on the Relationship Between the Old and New Testaments* (Wheaton, IL: Crossway Books, 1988).

CHAPTER 1
COVENANT IN SCRIPTURE

The term 'covenant' (*berit* in OT; *diathēkē* in NT) in Scripture is used for a "diversity of oath-bound commitments in various relationships."[2] This diversity of usage makes the term difficult to define. This book will only focus on the six major divine-human covenants. Acknowledging the difficulty of providing a single definition for all the different types of covenants in the ancient world and in Scripture, theologian Michael Williams broadly describes covenant as "a relationship between persons, begun by the sovereign determination of the greater party, in which the greater commits himself to the lesser in the context of mutual loyalty, and in which mutual obligations serve as illustrations of that loyalty."[3]

---

[2] Peter J. Gentry, "Kingdom Through Covenant: Humanity as the Divine Image," *The Southern Baptist Journal of Theology* 12, no. 1 (Spring 2008): 16.

[3] Michael D. Williams, *Far As the Curse is Found* (Phillipsburg, NJ: P & R Publishing, 2005), 45-46. Paul R. Williamson defines covenant as "a solemn commitment, guaranteeing promises or obligations undertaken by one or both parties, sealed with an oath," in *Sealed with an Oath: Covenant in God's Unfolding Plan* (Downers Grove, IL: InterVarsity Press, 2007), 43. Stephen Dempster writes that a covenant "refers to an agreement made between two parties," in *Dominion and Dynasty* (Downers Grove, IL: InterVarsity Press, 2003), 73.

Old Testament theologian Paul Williamson writes, "Covenant is without doubt one of the most important motifs in biblical theology, attested to not only by the traditional labels applied to the respective parts of the Christian Bible, but also by the fact that the concept looms large at important junctures throughout the Bible."[4] While covenant should not be considered the center of biblical theology, it is an important theological theme that illustrates at least one significant way in which the Bible's numerous and diverse voices unite with beautiful harmony.[5] Furthermore, it is erroneous to speak of covenant in the singular since there are several covenants. The six divine-human covenants this book has in mind are the following:

- Covenant with Creation (Gen 1-3)
- Covenant with Noah (Gen 6-9)
- Covenant with Abraham (Gen 12, 15, 17)
- Mosaic Covenant (Exod 19:3b-8, 20-24)
- Covenant with David (2 Sam 7, Ps 89)
- New Covenant (Jer 31:31-34, Ezek 33:29-39:29)[6]

---

[4] Williamson, *Sealed with an Oath*, 29.

[5] Ibid., 19, 32. Craig Bartholomew writes, "If one imagines the Bible as an edifice with many entrances, then I am not sure that covenant is *the* main entrance. I do think, though, that it is one of the main entrances, and that one gets a unified and overall picture from this entrance," in "Covenant and Creation: Covenant Overload or Covenant Deconstruction," *Calvin Theological Journal* 30, no. 1 (April 1995): 32.

[6] Gentry, "Kingdom Through Covenant," 19.

Reformed Covenant Theology has argued that all the covenants are different applications of the one covenant of grace made to Adam and Eve in the garden.[7] So the new covenant in their theological system is not really new, but renewed: a new administration of the one covenant of grace. While agreeing that there is much continuity between the various covenants, an over-arching covenant of grace as a theological category fails to do justice to the biblical texts. It is more faithful to the text to speak of the one plan of God (Eph 1.10),[8] with the biblical covenants forming the "backbone" of the biblical metanarrative, providing the key to the inner-literary structure of the Text.[9]

---

[7] "There are not therefore two covenants of grace, differing in substance, but one and the same, under various dispensations," *Westminster Confession of Faith* 7.6. For a modern exposition of Reformed Covenant Theology, see Michael Horton, *God of Promise: Introducing Covenant Theology* (Grand Rapids, MI: Baker Books, 2006).

[8] Jeffrey J. Niehaus uses the term "one divine program of revelation," in "An Argument Against Theologically Constructed Covenants," *Journal of the Evangelical Theological Society* 50, no. 2 (June 2007): 267. Williamson prefers to refer to "God's universal purpose – a purpose that is given clear expression in the Genesis creation narratives, and that finds its ultimate fulfillment in the new creation inaugurated through the death and resurrection of the Lord Jesus Christ," in *Sealed with an Oath*, 31.

[9] Gentry, "Kingdom Through Covenant," 19, 39 n.13. Williamson rightly calls covenant "a most important bonding agent

---

in the cement that unites Scripture as a whole," in *Sealed with an Oath*, 13.

CHAPTER 2
OLD TESTAMENT BACKGROUND

COVENANT WITH CREATION

Before examining the new covenant, the OT background must be considered. Creation is the obvious and all-important beginning point of the inscripturated Text. Out of his free and sovereign self-sufficiency, God created the heavens and earth, and created humans in his image (Gen 1:26-27).[10] While "covenant" does not occur in the opening chapters of Genesis, many have seen an implicit covenant in these chapters, though the matter is much debated. While not affirming the Reformed notion of a covenant of works or grace in Genesis 1-3, the evidence does demonstrate the viability of a covenant with creation in these chapters. William Dumbrell in particular has convincingly shown the presence of a covenant with crea-

---

[10] The notion of image would have been familiar in the Ancient Near East. The first hearers would have heard Yahweh making a grand statement. Greg Beale writes, "Ancient kings would set up images of themselves in distant lands over which they ruled in order to represent their sovereign presence. ...Likewise, Adam was created as the image of the divine king to indicate that earth was ruled over by Yahweh," in *The Temple and the Church's Mission: A Biblical Theology of the Dwelling Place of God* (Downers Grove, IL: InterVarsity Press, 2004), 82. All humanity was created in *his* image. Every time a person sees a person who is God's image, one should think, "God owns the world." This would have conveyed to the ancient mind that Yahweh alone is Ruler and Lord of the universe!

tion.[11] A key text is Genesis 6:18a, which reads, "But I will establish my covenant with you." This is the first time the word *covenant* is used in Genesis, but does this mean that the Noahic Covenant is the first in the storyline? Dumbrell has shown that covenant initiation is usually described by the words "cut a covenant." The absence of the standard terminology is due to the fact that Genesis 6:18 is not referring to the initiation of a new covenant, but rather a "confirmation of what was in fact an existing covenant."[12] There already existed a divine relationship that

---

[11] See his *Covenant and Creation: A Theology of the Old Testament Covenants* (Carlisle: Paternoster Press, 1984), especially 25-43; idem, *The Search for Order: Biblical Eschatology in Focus* (Eugene, OR: Wipf and Stock Publishers, 2001), 30-32. Also see J. V. Fesko, *Last Things First: Unlocking Genesis 1-3 with the Christ of Eschatology* (Scotland: Mentor, 2007), 82-95; Williams, *Far As the Curse*, 45ff; Jeffrey J. Niehaus, *God At Sinai* (Grand Rapids, MI: Zondervan, 1995), 143-50.

[12] Dumbrell, *Covenant and Creation*, 43. Unfortunately, on the same page Dumbrell writes, "There could be only one biblical covenant, of which the later biblical covenants must be sub-sets." Scott Hafemann (a Baptist!) similarly flattens out the various covenants by arguing for a single covenant relationship in "The Covenant Relationship," in *Central Themes in Biblical Theology* ed. by Scott J. Hafemann and Paul R. House (Grand Rapids: Baker Academic, 2007), 20-65. There is not *one* covenant relationship, but many with significant progression between them. In *The Search for Order*, Dumbrell writes, "In every case where 'establish a covenant' occurs, the phrase refers, not to the initiation of the covenant, but to the perpetuation of a covenant previously concluded (cf. Gen. 17:7, 19, 21; Exod. 6:4; Lev. 26:9; Deut. 8:18; 2 Kings 23:3; Jer. 34:18). We may surmise then that the phrase 'estab-

was established by creation itself, which is confirmed with Noah.[13] Noah should be seen as a new Adam with a new start, who is given the same commission to be fruitful, multiply, and fill the earth (Gen 1:28, 9:1, 7).

Hosea 6:7a is also an important but debated text that says, "But like Adam they transgressed the covenant." This seems to point toward an Adamic or creational covenant. Additionally, in Jeremiah, the Lord speaks of the covenant with the day and with night, echoing the words of Genesis (Jer 33:19-26). Michael D. Williams writes, "In the midst of exile, the prophet reassures Israel that God's faithfulness to his people is as sure as his faithfulness to his creation. As God has covenantally bound himself to creation, he has no less bound himself to Israel."[14] All this points to the fact that "God's creative activity is covenantal."[15]

It is also very significant that the New Testament never mentions a typological relationship between Christ and

---

lish my covenant' in Genesis 6:18 (and in Gen. 9:9, 11, 17) refers to the maintenance of a preexisting *covenant* relationship," 31.

[13] Ibid., 32. Also see Gentry's penetrating theological and linguistic argument for a covenant with creation, made at creation in "Kingdom Through Covenant," 16-22.

[14] Williams, Far As the Curse, 47.

[15] Fesko, *Last Things First,* 84. Similarly, Dumbrell writes, "any theology of covenant must begin with Genesis 1:1," in *Covenant and Creation,* 42.

Noah.[16] All later covenants have their foundation with creation. Scripture is replete with allusions to a new Adam, new creation, and new Edenic situation. This should be clear from a careful reading of the storyline. Adam is commissioned, but claiming moral and epistemological autonomy, fails to bow to the Creator in all areas of life. The consequences of this 'cosmic tragedy'[17] are immediately discernable with the murder of Abel. Noah is called out by grace as a new Adam, but then we find Genesis 3 all over again with Noah's drunkenness. Although humanity was wicked before and after the flood, God remains committed to his creation and faithful to his covenant. Israel is called out, but falls with the golden calf incident before the covenant is even ratified. Adam's failure as federal[18] head has consequences for the entire human race. Now everyone born is born "in Adam." His disobedience brings death on all humankind,[19] but God promised the woman that she would bring forth a descendent who, though being bruised, would crush the head of the serpent (Gen 3:15). Finally,

---

[16] Concerning Paul Williamson, who denies a covenant with creation, Peter Gentry writes, "The metanarrative constructed by Williamson is one essentially beginning with Noah in which Adam has largely disappeared. This damages the parallels Paul draws between Adam and Christ," in "Kingdom Through Covenant," 21.

[17] Dempster, Dominion and Dynasty, 66.

[18] "Federal" is simply a derivative of the Latin term *foedus*, which means covenant.

[19] See Anthony A. Hoekema, *Created in God's Image* (Grand Rapids: Eerdmans, 1986), 133ff.

the thesis of this book is not dependent on the argument for a covenant with creation. Although lacking covenant terminology, a covenant framework in Genesis 1-3 is certainly conceptually appropriate.[20] At the very least, Genesis 1-3 should be considered covenant-like, and it must always be emphasized that God is committed to his creation.

NOAHIC COVENANT

God was fed up with sinful humanity, so he sent the rain of judgment to flood the earth, reversing the creation (Gen 1:6-9, 7:17-24), but God was not finished with his creation so he called out Noah as a new Adam. Genesis 3:15 will now be realized through Noah's seed.[21] Stephen Dempster writes, "The covenant with creation after the flood uses language extremely similar to that of Gen. 1-2 [cf. Gen 1:28, 9:1, 7], even though the word *covenant* does

---

[20] Brian J. Vickers, *Jesus' Blood and Righteousness: Paul's Theology of Imputation* (Wheaton, IL: Crossway Books, 2006), 150-51.

[21] On the importance of "seed," see T.D. Alexander, "Genealogies, Seed and the Compositional Unity of Genesis," *Tyndale Bulletin* 44.2 (November 1993): 255-70; idem, "Royal Expectations in Genesis to Kings: The Importance for Biblical Theology," *Tyndale Bulletin* 49.2 (November 1998):191-212; idem, "Seed," in *New Dictionary of Biblical Theology*, ed. T. Desmond Alexander, et al. (Downers Grove, IL: InterVarsity Press, 2000), 769-73; John G. Reisinger, *Abraham's Four Seeds: A Biblical Examination of the Presuppositions of Covenant Theology and Dispensationalism* (Frederick, MD: New Covenant Media, 1998).

not occur there.[22] The 'new' covenant with creation is not quite like the old, as there are significant flaws in the post-flood world."[23] It was noted above that the phrase "establish my covenant" (Gen 6:18) refers to a pre-existing covenant relationship, but if one is not convinced by the arguments for a covenant with creation, then the Noahic Covenant at least confirms the divine intention expressed in creation.[24] Even though the intention of man's heart was still wicked, God promises to never again baptize the earth with the chaotic waters (Gen 8:21). As a sign of the covenant, Yahweh placed his bow in the clouds pointing up towards him, laying down his weapon of war. While God had every right to destroy and start anew, he decides to conquer in *this* world.[25]

---

[22] Contra Williamson, who writes, "These echoes [of the creation narrative in the Noahic covenant] suggest merely that God intended, through Noah, to fulfill his original creative intent; they do not necessarily presuppose the existence of a covenant between God and inanimate creation or indicate that the material in Genesis 1-3 must be understood covenantally," in *Sealed with an Oath*, 75.

[23] Dempster, *Dominion and Dynasty*, 73 n.34. Similarly, Dumbrell writes, "The pledge by God after the flood to maintain the created order (Gen 8:21), which is the substance of the covenant affirmation to Noah, seems to refer to a divine commitment to preserve the structure of creation that was given implicitly to humankind by the act of creation itself," in *Search for Order*, 31.

[24] Blaising and Bock, *Progressive Dispensationalism*, 129, 151.

[25] I owe this insight to Peter J. Gentry.

ABRAHAMIC COVENANT

In Genesis 12, "the Bible's Magna Carta,"[26] Abram, a sort of new Adam, is called from darkness to light (Josh 24:2) as a "divine reply to the human disaster of Genesis 3-11."[27] Genesis 12:1-3 says, "Now the Lord said to Abram, 'Go from your country and your kindred and your father's house to the land that I will show you. And I will make of you a great nation, and I will bless you and make your name great, so that you will be a blessing. I will bless those who bless you, and him who dishonors you I will curse, and in you all the families of the earth shall be blessed.'" God calls a new phase of history into being and promises Abram land, seed, and blessing (Gen 12 – the real content of the covenant).[28] Darrell Bock and Craig Blaising write, "The Abrahamic covenant consequently sets forth the foundational relationship between God and all humankind from Abraham onward. This means that to understand the Bible, one must read it in view of the Abrahamic covenant, for that covenant with Abraham is the foundational framework for interpreting the Scripture

---

[26] Williamson, Sealed with an Oath, 77.

[27] Dumbrell, *Search for Order*, 34. Dumbrell also writes, "The covenant with Abraham is a response to the situation created by the fall, remotely, and immediately to the circumstances arising from the humanistic attempt by man to find the centre [sic] of his world in himself," in "The Covenant with Abraham," The Reformed Theological Review 41, no. 2 (May-August 1982): 50.

[28] Dumbrell, "The Covenant with Abraham," 50; idem, *Covenant and Creation*, 47.

and the history of redemption which it reveals."[29] The relationship begun in Genesis 12 is formalized in 15, where the slain animals are laid on the ground, and the Lord passes between the pieces while Abram was asleep (Gen 15:7-21 cf. Jer 34:18)! God takes the curse upon himself, saying in effect, "May what happened to these animals happen to me if I (or you) break the covenant. Little did Abram know that in the fullness of time, his true seed would indeed take the curse upon himself by being hanged on a tree (Gal 3:13-16). The covenant is confirmed, Abram's name is changed to Abraham, and the terms are

---

[29] Bock and Blaising, *Progressive Dispensationalism*, 135. Similarly, Dumbrell writes, "What is being offered in these verses is a theological blueprint for the redemptive history of the world, now set in train by the call of Abram, *Covenant and Creation*, 66. Cf. also, idem, "The Covenant with Abraham," 46. Stephen J. Wellum agrees, writing, "Scripture presents the Abrahamic covenant as the basis for all God's dealings with the human race and the backbone for understanding the biblical covenants. Truly, it is through Abraham and his seed—ultimately viewed in terms of our Lord Jesus Christ (Gal 3:16)—that our Triune God fulfills his eternal purpose and promise to save a people for himself and to usher in a new creation. This is borne out, not only in terms of OT theology, but also in how the NT authors interpret the fulfillment of the Abrahamic promise in light of the person and work of Christ (e.g. Romans 4 and Galatians 3)," in his excellent essay "Baptism and the Relationship Between the Covenants," in *Believer's Baptism*, ed. Thomas R. Schreiner and Shawn D. Wright (Nashville: B & H Academic, 2006), 128-29.

restated in chapter 17.[30] This covenant is clearly built off of the Noahic and creational covenants. Stephen Dempster writes, "God's programme [sic] with and through Abraham is to restore the original conditions of creation described in Genesis 1-2."[31]

MOSAIC COVENANT

The basis of Israel's calling is Yahweh's faithfulness to the patriarchs (Exod 2:24, 6:4-5), which is based on his faithfulness to creation. Israel emerges as a corporate Adam.[32] God promised to make Abraham a great nation

---

[30] Dumbrell writes, "Genesis 17 has operated as a consolidation of the Abrahamic covenant and as an extension of its detail. In this connection, material contained in chapters 12 and 15 is represented and summated," in Covenant and Creation, 74. Also see idem, Search for Order, 35. Against Williamson (Sealed with an Oath, 77-93 who argues for two covenants with Abraham (15 & 17)), "there is no theological development of the concept berit in Gen. 17. That chapter is merely a reaffirmation of the material of Gen. 12 and 15," in Covenant and Creation, 77.

[31] Dempster, Dominion and Dynasty, 79. Bock and Blaising similarly write, "Like the Noahic covenant, the Abrahamic covenant stands in contrast to the judgments of God on human sin and presents anew the plan of creation," in Progressive Dispensationalism, 130.

[32] D.A Carson writes, "We must not forget that the story of the nation of Israel is itself embedded into the larger story of Abraham and his seed (a point made by Paul in Galatians 3), which is itself embedded into the still larger story of the creation and fall of the human race (a point made by Paul in

(*goy*),[33] so Sinai can be clearly seen as *dependent* upon, and as an *advance on*, the Abrahamic Covenant.[34] God delivers Israel from Egypt and makes a covenant with them at Sinai. God has redeemed Israel, and they in turn must trust in him with all their lives. How do they trust? By obeying the stipulations given at Sinai (Exod 19:5-6). This covenant, unlike the previous ones, is marked by specific conditions for each party. The purpose of the covenant is that God's son, Israel (Exod 4:22), may bring God's rule and creation blessing to the surrounding nations. They are to be Yahweh's "treasured possession among all peoples, for all the earth is mine; and you shall be to me a kingdom of

---

Romans 1:18-3:32; 5:1-19)," in *Christ & Culture Revisited* (Grand Rapids, MI: Eerdmans, 2008), 52. In the context of reflecting on the chronological sequence of the Tanakh, Dempster writes that "Israel's national history is subordinated to that of world history," in *Dominion and Dynasty*, 23. Also note the language of commission: 1:28, 9:1, 9:7, 12:2f, 17:2,6,8, 22:16f, 26:3f, 26:24, 28:3, 35:11f. 47:27, 48:3f.

[33] Dumbrell writes, "The usual term applied to Israel is Heb. *am* 'people', a kinship term which expresses effectively the closeness of the relationship between God and Israel which Israel's election had established. We would thus need to ask ourselves why *goy* would have been considered an appropriate term here. It could be readily argued that what is in mind is the emergence of Israel as a political unit at a later stage and that the qualifier 'great' in Gen. 12:2 sets her off from her world," in *Covenant and Creation*, 66.

[34] Wellum, "Relationship Between the Covenants," 130; Dumbrell, *Covenant and Creation*, 87-89; Bock and Blaising, *Progressive Dispensationalism*, 140-49; Williamson, *Sealed with an Oath*, 94-96.

priests and a holy nation," (Exod 19:5-6). Israel was to be true humanity, in right relationship with God, community, and creation, exercising good stewardship of all the earth's resources. Israel's dominion was to be characterized by service.[35] Of course Israel, like Adam and Noah, failed to please God, breaking the covenant before it was even formally established (Exod 32)! Indeed, Israel was unable to serve the Lord (Josh 24:19), lacking the heart inclined to keep the Torah (Deut 30:6, 31:16). It will be shown below that God's intention was for the Mosaic administration to be an *interim* administration.

DAVIDIC COVENANT

Second Samuel 7 is considered "one of the most important chapters in the Hebrew Bible."[36] It contains God's covenant with David, which is most certainly built on the previous covenants (also see 1 Chron 17, Ps 89, 110, 132).[37] While containing the trajectory of the Sinai covenant,[38] the

---

[35] Dempster, Dominion and Dynasty, 101-02.

[36] Ibid., 142.

[37] Though covenant is not used in 2 Sam 7, it is clearly perceived as such throughout the rest of the canon. Cf. 2 Sam 23:5, Ps 89:3, 28, 34, 132:11, Isa 55:3.

[38] The *sonship* terms previously applied to Adam (Gen 1:26-27, 5:1-3, Luke 3:23, 38) and to Israel (Exod 4:22, Hos 11:1) are now applied to the Davidic king (2 Sam 7:14, Ps 2). Peter Gentry writes, "A canonical reading indicates that the Davidic King is inheriting both the role of Adam as son of God and Israel as son of God according to the instructions of Deut 17," in "Rethinking the 'Sure Mercies of David' in

Davidic covenant is most closely aligned with the Abrahamic covenant. For example, both Abraham and David are promised a great name (Gen 12:2, 2 Sam 7:9), victory over their enemies (Gen 22:17, 2 Sam 7:11, Ps 89:23), a special divine-human relationship (Gen 17:7-8, 2 Sam 7:24, Ps 89:26), a place for God's people (Gen 12:1, 2 Sam 7:10), and a line of descendents through which their name would be perpetuated (Gen 21:12, 2 Sam 7:12-16). Both must keep God's law (Gen 18:19, 2 Sam 7:14, Ps 89:30-32, 132:12), and a unique "seed" of both would mediate international blessing (Gen 22:18, Ps 72:17).[39] The Abrahamic promises will be realized through the Davidic dynasty (Gen 17:6).[40] Bock and Blaising write, "The blessing for the many will be mediated by the rulership of the one, the king."[41] One must also keep in mind that even the Abrahamic covenant is rooted in the Noahic and creation co-

---

Isaiah 55:3," *Westminster Theological Journal* 69.2, (Fall 2007): 286. So also Wellum, "The Relationship Between the Covenants," 131. Also note that David and Moses are called God's "servant" (Josh 1:1, 24:29, 2 Sam 7: 5, 8).

[39] Williamson, Sealed with an Oath, 144. Also cf. Dumbrell, Covenant and Creation, 149; Dempster, Dominion and Dynasty, 142-43.

[40] Andreas J. Kostenberger and Peter T. O'Brien write, "2 Samuel 7 [esp. vv. 9-11] contains important allusions to Genesis 12:1-3 which suggest that what God has in store for David is a *reiteration*, if not a *partial fulfillment*, of what was promised to Abraham," in *Salvation to the Ends of the Earth: A Biblical Theology of Mission* (Downers Grove, IL: InterVarsity Press, 2001), 39.

[41] Bock and Blaising, *Progressive Dispensationalism*, 166.

venants (or *at least* God's intention in creation).[42] Dempster writes, "David is a new Adam appointed as God's
vicegerent over the world to subdue it and have dominion over it,"[43] showing that it will be the Davidic ruler
who will crush the serpent's head (Gen 3:15).

The covenant with David consists of two main parts:
the promise to build the Davidic house and the promise
of a special relationship with David's son.[44] We see in the
immediate context in David's prayer of gratitude (2 Sam
7:18-29) that "he well understood this covenantal significance of the divine promises and their effect upon humanity as a whole."[45] Second Samuel 7:19b says, "You have
spoken also of your servant's house for a great while to
come, and this is instruction for mankind." The promise

---

[42] Stephen Wellum writes, "Thus, under the Davidic king, the
Abrahamic promise of the great nation and great name
come together. In this sense, the ultimate fulfillment of the
Abrahamic covenant coincides with the ultimate fulfillment
of the Davidic covenant. The Abrahamic blessings, linked
back to Noah and creation, will only be ultimately realized
through the Davidic son. Indeed, the final fulfillment of the
Abrahamic promise of blessing in a promised land will take
place under the rulership of the Davidic king. In this important sense, the Davidic king becomes the mediator of covenant blessing, tied back to Abraham, ultimately tied back to
Adam, as the covenant head of the human race," in "The Relationship Between the Covenants," 131.

[43] Dempster, *Dominion and Dynasty*, 198. See also Kostenberger,
Salvation to the Ends, 40; Dumbrell, *Search for Order*, 72-73.

[44] Bock and Blaising, *Progressive Dispensationalism*, 159-60.

[45] Dumbrell, *Covenant and Creation*, 151.

just given to David is to be the "charter for humanity."[46]
David understands the dynastic promises have ramifications far beyond the borders of Israel. These promises are tied to God's creational blessing (Gen 1-2, 9) and international blessing for all humanity through Abraham (Gen 12).[47] In the ancient Near Eastern and Canaanite cultural context, the kings were perceived as the image of god because he was the son of god. The king would represent the character of the god in some way to the surrounding people. A country or region was thought to be ruled by the local god of that region, and the king was the representative of that god. As with God's intention in the garden with Adam as the divine image and son (Gen 1:26-27, 5:1-3, Luke 3:23, 38, see note 10), the Davidic king/son (2 Sam 7:14, Ps 2:7) was to image or represent the rule of Yahweh to the nation of Israel and the surrounding nations. But unlike the pagan gods of local regions, the God that the Davidic king represents is the exclusive Lord of the *cosmos*. Hence, the covenant with David is the charter for all humanity.[48] Indeed, the Davidic king is "the highest of the kings of the earth" with world-wide implications (Ps 89:27), having dominion from sea to sea (Ps 72:8, Ps 2:8)!

---

[46] Walter C. Kaiser, Jr., "The Blessing of David: The Charter for Humanity," in *The Law and the Prophets*, ed. John H. Skilton (Nutley, NJ: Presbyterian and Reformed Publishing Co., 1974), 298-318; Also cf. Dumbrell *Search for Order*, 72; idem, *Covenant and Creation*, 151-52.

[47] Ibid., 314; Williamson, *Sealed with an Oath*, 129; Dumbrell, *Search for Order*, 72.

[48] Gentry, "Rethinking the Sure Mercies of David," 284-88.

God's promise (rooted in his faithfulness to creation) to raise up a descendent is unconditional, but a continuous, uninterrupted rein is conditioned upon the faithfulness of the Davidic line.[49] Peter Gentry shows that it is not quite accurate to call it unconditional because there are clear conditions in 2 Samuel 7:14-15, but the conditions are supported on both sides (11b-13 and 16) by the faithfulness and sure promises of God to David of descendents, a kingdom, and a throne.[50] Solomon would be the expected descendent, but he literally turns Deuteronomy 17 upside down with his disobedient rule. An obedient David is needed, and the rest of the storyline of Scripture repeats the hope that God will provide a faithful David. Psalm 132 is a prayer for God to keep his oath to David based upon an obedient David (Ps 132:10-12, cf. 2 Chron 6:41-42).[51] God will make an everlasting covenant based on the

---

[49] Bock and Blaising, *Progressive Dispensationalism*, 164; Kostenberger, *Salvation to the Ends*, 38. Dumbrell notes, "Though the line will not fail, covenantal promises may be withdrawn from individuals in David's house. In physical terms the Davidic line failed when Jerusalem fell to Nebuchadnezzar in 587/586 B.C., but in spiritual terms Jesus of Nazareth eschatologically consummates the promises given to the house of David," in *Search for Order*, 71.

[50] Gentry, "Rethinking the Sure Mercies of David," 283.

[51] Ibid., 292. Gentry shows that "For the sake of your servant David" (Ps 132:10) is best rendered "on account of what David has done."

acts of loyal love performed by the future Davidic servant king (Isa 9:6-7, 11:1-2, 53-55, esp. 55:3, Acts 13:34).[52]

NEW COVENANT

Allusions and prophecies about the new covenant are abundant in the OT,[53] but Jeremiah 31 is *the* crucial passage for our understanding of the new covenant. The new covenant passage (31:31-34) is preceded by a short but important proverb: "In those days they shall no longer say: 'The fathers have eaten sour grapes, and the children's teeth are set on edge.' But everyone shall die for his own sin. Each man who eats sour grapes, his teeth shall be set on edge" (31:29-30). This proverb refers to the "tribal" nature of the old covenant. During the Mosaic era, only Israel's leaders (usually prophets, priests, and kings) were bestowed with the Spirit.[54] As the leaders went, so went the nation (Josh 9:18). Stephen Wellum writes,

---

[52] Ibid., 279-304; Also Dempster, *Dominion and Dynasty*, 180-81.

[53] E.g. Ezek 11:19-20, 36:26-27, 37:14, 39:29, Joel 2:28-29, Deut 30:6, Jer 32:39-40, Isa 32:15, 44:3, 55:3, 54:13. The new covenant is also referred to as the everlasting covenant (Jer 32:36-41, 50:2-5, Ezek 16:59-63, 37:15-28, Isa 24:5, 55:1-5, 61:8-9), the covenant of peace (Isa 54:1-10, Ezek 34:20-31, 37:15-28), and promises of a new heart and new spirit (Ezek 11:18-21, 18:30-32, 36:24-32.

[54] See James M. Hamilton, Jr., *God's Indwelling Presence: The Holy Spirit in the Old and New Testaments* (Nashville, TN: B&H Academic, 2006), 27-34. In his conclusion to that chapter, Hamilton writes, "The Spirit came on such people to differentiate them from the rest of the nation and empower them for their task," 55.

Despite remnant themes and an emphasis on individual believers, the OT pictures God working with his people as a "tribal" grouping whose knowledge of God and whose relations with God were uniquely dependent on specially endowed leaders. Thus, the strong emphasis on the Spirit of God being poured out, not on each believer, but distinctively on prophets, priests, kings, and a few designated special leaders (e.g., Bezalel). Given this hierarchical structure of the covenant community, when these leaders did what was right, the entire nation benefited. However, when they did not, the entire nation suffered for their actions.[55]

But changes are coming in the latter days as God promises that he will make a new covenant with his people, *not like*[56] "the covenant that I made with their fathers on the

---

[55] Wellum, "Relationship Between the Covenants," 142; Also see D.A Carson, *Showing the Spirit: A Theological Exposition of 1 Corinthians 12-14* (Grand Rapids, MI: Baker Books, 1987), 151-53; idem, "Evangelicals, Ecumenism and the Church," in *Evangelical Affirmations*, ed. Kenneth S. Kantzer and Carl F.H. Henry (Grand Rapids, MI: Academie Books, 1990), 359-63; Thomas R. Schreiner, *New Testament Theology: Magnifying God in Christ* (Grand Rapids, MI: Baker Academic, 2008), 432.

[56] Femi Adeyemi writes concerning this phrase that it is "an emphatic negation. The phrase underscores the complete dissimilarity of this New Covenant with the old Sinaitic Covenant. This phrase does not suggest a mere renewal of the Mosaic Covenant," in "What Is The New Covenant 'Law' In Jeremiah 31:33?," *Bibliotheca Sacra* 163, no. 651 (July-September 2006): 319; Also see Williamson, *Sealed with an Oath*, 152f; Contra Dumbrell, who writes, "The 'new' covenant appears to have had in mind a fresh dispensation of the

day when I took them by the hand to bring them out of the land of Egypt, my covenant that they broke," (31:32), clearly referring to the Mosaic covenant. Yahweh promises to put his law within them and write it on their hearts. He will be their God and they shall be his people. It will no longer be a mixed community of some spiritually circumcised and others only physically circumcised (Jer 9:25-26), "for they shall all know me, from the least of them to the greatest, declares the Lord. For I will forgive their iniquity and I will remember their sin no more" (31:34). Carson writes, "In short, Jeremiah understood that the new covenant would bring some dramatic changes. The tribal nature of the people of God would end, and the new covenant would bring with it a new emphasis on the distribution of the knowledge of God down to the level of each member of the covenant community."[57]

Sinai covenant, or better, a re-writing of the provisions of the Sinai covenant on the individual heart," *Covenant and Creation,* 199, 180-81; idem, *Search for Order,* 98, 325; idem, *The End of the Beginning* (Eugene, OR: Wipf and Stock Publishers, 2001), 92; Hafemann, "The Covenant Relationship," 50-51. Jason C. Meyer has shown that Hafemann (who follows Dumbrell) "fails to account for the christological newness of the new covenant and its corresponding relationship to the pneumatological dimension of the new covenant." The new covenant is "qualitatively superior," in "Paul, the Mosaic Covenant, and Redemptive History" (Ph.D. diss., The Southern Baptist Theological Seminary, 2007), 123-28.

[57] Carson, *Showing the Spirit,* 152; Hafemann, "The Covenant Relationship," 54-55; Thomas R. Schreiner, "The Commands of God," in *Central Themes in Biblical Theology* ed. by Scott J.

Similarly, Ezekiel prophesies that Yahweh will give his people a new heart and a new spirit. The heart of stone will be removed and replaced with a heart of flesh, and God will put his Spirit within them and cause them to walk in his statutes and be careful to obey his rules (Ezek 36:26-27).[58] Moses' desire that the Lord would put his Spirit on all his people (Num 11:29) will become a reality in the new covenant era. Joel had also prophesied that the Lord would pour out his Spirit on all flesh (Joel 2:28-29). The messianic age would be the age of the Spirit.[59] The enabling power of the Spirit would produce two loyal parties instead of one.[60] The new Israel would be an obedient Israel due to the universal distribution of the Spirit to all members of the covenant community, which will include Jews *and Gentiles* (Jer 33:19, Ezek 36:36, 37:28, Isa 42:6, 49:6, 55:3-5, 56:4-8, 66:18-24)! So the new covenant announced in the OT is not only a temporal advance in redemptive history, but also a qualitative and eschatolog-

---

Hafemann and Paul R. House (Grand Rapids: Baker Academic, 2007), 75.

[58] For more on this verse and the new covenant, see Hamilton, *God's Indwelling Presence,* 48-55.

[59] See Wellum, "Baptism and the Relationship Between the Covenants," 143; Beale, *The Temple and the Church's Mission,* 209-12; Schreiner, *New Testament Theology,* 433; Carson, "Evangelicals, Ecumenism, & the Church," 362-63; idem, *Showing the Spirit,* 153. Also see Ezek 11:19, 37:, 14 with allusions to Gen 2:7 and new creation, 39:29, Isa 32:15, 44:3, 59:21.

[60] Dumbrell, The End of the Beginning, 90.

ical advance.[61] The new covenant is also radically new in
that it will be unbreakable, unlike the old covenant.[62] The
new era will be the age of full and final forgiveness. Jeremiah 31:34b says, "For I will forgive their iniquity, and I
will remember their sin no more." Remembering sin was
inevitable and unending under the old covenant sacrificial system. Dumbrell writes, "In the context of Jer. 31:34
for God 'not to remember' means that no action will need
to be taken in the new age against sin."[63] In saying this,
Jeremiah anticipates the cessation of the old covenant sacrificial system.[64] Hafemann summarizes well: "The
foundation of the covenant is forgiveness; the provision of
the covenant is the Spirit; the consequence of the covenant
is obedience; the promise of the covenant is to be in God's
presence forever as his faithful people."[65]

---

[61] Kostenberger, Salvation to the Ends of the Earth, 43.

[62] Williamson, Sealed with an Oath, 157; Dumbrell, The End of
the Beginning, 90.

[63] Dumbrell, The End of the Beginning, 94; idem, Covenant and
Creation, 182.

[64] Williamson, Sealed with an Oath, 157.

[65] Hafemann, Scott J, *Second Corinthians,* in *The NIV Application
Commentary,* ed. Terry Muck, (Grand Rapids, MI: Zondervan, 2000), 136.

CHAPTER 3
NEW TESTAMENT

The NT presents Christ as fulfilling all the promises of God in their initial stage. "For all the promises of God find their Yes in him" (2 Cor 1:20). Jesus himself asserts that the OT Scriptures bear witness about him (John 5:39). Luke 24:27 says, "Beginning with Moses and all the Prophets, he interpreted to them in all the Scriptures the things concerning himself" (cf. John 1:45, Heb 1:1, Luke 1:54-55). Jesus is presented as the last Adam (1 Cor 15:21, 45, Rom 5:12-21),[66] the true seed of Abraham (Gal 3:16), the new Moses (Num 12:7-8, Deut 18:15-18, 34:10, Matt 5, John 1, Acts 3:22, 7:37, Heb 3:1-6),[67] the true Israel (Matt 2:15, 4:1-11, John 15:1),[68] David's greater Son (Matt 1:1-17, Acts 2:29-36, Rev 22:16),[69] who will not only rule over eth-

---

[66] Schreiner, *New Testament Theology*, 307-08; Also see my "Christ as the Last Adam," *Adorare Mente* 1 (Spring 2008), 30-42.

[67] Frank Thielman, *The Law and the New Testament: The Question of Continuity* (New York: The Crossroad Publishing Company, 1999), 179. Also see idem, *Theology of the New Testament: A Canonical and Synthetic Approach* (Grand Rapids, MI: Zondervan, 2005), 91-93; Schreiner, *New Testament Theology*, 173-75.

[68] N.T Wright, *The Climax of the Covenant* (Minneapolis: Fortress Press, 1993), 18-40; Also see Schreiner, *New Testament Theology*, 73, 236f.

[69] See Schreiner, *New Testament Theology*, 199-201. For a great treatment of Scripture's portrait of the Messiah, see T.D. Al-

nic Jews in a piece of land in the East, but is king of the cosmos (Ps 89:27, 2 Sam 7:19, Matt 5:5, Heb 11:10, Rom 4:13),[70] ruling over a reconstituted and fully forgiven Israel consisting of Jews and Gentiles (Gal 6:16) as mediator of the Abrahamic promises of seed, land, and blessing to his new humanity (Eph 2:11-22).

Christ also, by his life, death, resurrection, and ascension, ratified the *radically new* covenant, which all the other covenants anticipated and foreshadowed.[71] Dumbrell writes, "Given an eschatological setting, Jesus' death constitutes the decisive eon-changing event."[72] He is the faithful covenant head, unlike all the previous covenant mediators who failed to fulfill the covenant requirements. Unlike God's previous sons: Adam (Gen 1:28, 5:1, Luke 3:38), Israel (Exod 4:22, Hos 11:1, Ezek 37), and David's

---

exander, *The Servant King* (Vancouver: Regent College Publishing, 1998).

[70] See Douglas J. Moo, "Nature in the New Creations: New Testament Eschatology and the Environment," *Journal of the Evangelical Theological Society* 49, no. 3 (September 2006): 458-69; Williamson, *Sealed with an Oath*, 192.

[71] Williamson writes, "Thus the new covenant is the climactic fulfillment of the covenants that God established with the patriarchs, the nation of Israel, and the dynasty of David. The promises of these earlier covenants find their ultimate fulfillment in this new covenant, and in it such promises become 'eternal' in the truest sense," in *Sealed with an Oath*, 181.

[72] Dumbrell, *Search for Order*, 271. Similarly, Thielman writes that the cross of Christ "split the ages in two," in *Theology of the New Testament*, 267.

sons (2 Sam 7:14), God is well pleased with this Son (Matt 3:17). God is also well pleased with the "corporate Christ," i.e. those who are united to Christ by faith.[73] For Christ is the propitiation for all who trust him, who are counted righteous in him, a grace gift that is now available in this new age apart from the law covenant (Rom 3:21).[74] The previous covenant mediators pointed forward to Christ, the truly faithful covenant head who brings eschatological advance and massive changes. Jesus is presented as the unique bearer of the Spirit (Isa 11:1-5, Luke 3:22) who brings about the messianic age of the Spirit (Isa 61:1-2, Luke 4:17-21), indicating "that God is beginning to fulfill the saving promises made to Abraham."[75] At Pentecost (Acts 2), the birthday of the church and inauguration of new covenant blessing, the promises of the democratization of the Spirit and full forgiveness of sin (Joel 2, Jer 31) becomes a reality.[76] Once Jesus had been glorified

---

[73] C.F.D Moule, *The Phenomenon of the New Testament* (London: SCM Press, 1967), 21-42. Also see Schreiner, *New Testament Theology*, 308, 316.

[74] See D.A. Carson, "Atonement in Romans 3:21-26," in *The Glory of the Atonement*, ed. Charles E. Hill and Frank A. James III (Downers Grove, IL: 2004), 119-39.

[75] Schreiner, *New Testament Theology*, 23, 29. Schreiner also writes, "The blessing pledged to Abraham (Gen. 12:3) is nothing less than the promise of the Spirit (Isa. 44:3), and this blessing now belongs to believers (Gal. 3:14), indicating that the last days have begun," 477, cf. also 33, 99, 431, 476, 505.

[76] Ibid., 734.

(John 7:37-39, 16:5-12), he sent the Spirit in full measure ensuring that *every last* member of the new covenant community will share in the Spirit, in union with Christ. We now turn to briefly examine several key NT passages.

GOSPELS

Jesus does not explicitly introduce the new covenant until late in the gospel narratives (Matt 26:28, Luke 22:20, Mark 14:24, cf. 1 Cor 11:25), but the gospels are full of teaching regarding the relationship between the OT and new age brought about by the coming of Christ. The prologue for John's Gospel is significant in this regard. John 1:14 says, "And the Word became flesh and dwelt among us, and we have seen his glory, glory as of the only Son from the Father, full of grace and truth" (cf. Exod 33-34). John uses "dwelt" (from *skēnoō* – "tabernacled") to show that God now dwells with his people through Jesus, the true temple (John 2:19-21).[77] From the fullness of Christ we have received grace instead (*anti*) of grace (1:16), "For the law was given through Moses; grace and truth came through Jesus Christ," (John 1:17). John is communicating

---

[77] D.A. Carson, *The Gospel According to John*, in *The Pillar New Testament Commentary*, ed. D.A. Carson (Grand Rapids, MI: Eerdmans, 1991), 127. For an excellent treatment of this theme, see Beale, *The Temple and the Church's Mission*. Concerning this verse, Dumbrell writes, "John thus depicts Jesus as the embodiment of the rule of God, as the replacement for the tabernacle of the exodus, as the true temple, that is, the new focus of true worship," in *Search for Order*, 239.

that the grace of the new covenant is superior to the grace
of the old covenant.[78]

Matthew, "where the Old and New Testaments meet,"
opens his Gospel with the assertion that Jesus is the anticipated Jewish King (1:1). Though many texts could be ap-
pealed to in this gospel,[79] Matthew 5:17ff is probably the
most important. Matthew 5:1 tells us that Jesus, like Moses receiving the Decalogue at Mount Sinai, "went up on
the mountain" to give a new law. In 5:17, Jesus says, "Do
not think that I have come to abolish the Law or the
Prophets; I have not come to abolish them but to fulfill
them." A study of this entire chapter is needed to do justice to verse 17, but space permits only a few probing
comments. "Law or the Prophets" clearly includes the old
covenant and probably refers to the entire Old Testament.
"Abolish" (*kataluō*) is fairly straight forward, meaning do
away with, abolish, or destroy. The controversial and important word in this text is "fulfill" (*plēroō*). Matthew uses
this term in a special way throughout his gospel (see note
79). This fact, coupled with the following context must be
considered before proposing an appropriate definition for
"fulfill" in verse 17. Verses 21-48 are of particular importance.[80] When Jesus says, "You have heard that it was said

[78] Schreiner, *New Testament Theology,* 642; Carson, *John,* 132.

[79] See Matthew 1:1-17, 1:22, 2:15, 2:16-18, 2:19-23, 3:17, 4:14, 5:17,
8:17, 9:17, 10, 11:13, 12:17, 13:35, 17:1f, 21:4, 24, 26:54-56, 27:9.

[80] For detailed exegesis of these verses, see Douglas J. Moo, "Jesus and the Authority of the Mosaic Law," *Journal for the
Study of the New Testament* 20 (1984): 3-49; D.A. Carson, *Matthew,* Vol. 1. in *The Expositors Bible Commentary,* ed. Frank E.

to those of old," (v. 21) "it is difficult to exclude some reference to the generation who received the law at Sinai."[81] Jesus goes on to contrast what was heard in the past with what he demands as the sovereign interpreter of the law. The emphatic "But I say to you," and the various antitheses show that the teaching of Jesus is not simply interpreting the true intention of the Mosaic law,[82] but rather advancing and even contravening it at points.[83]

What then can Jesus mean by saying that he did not come to abolish the Law and the Prophets? Jesus advances and even contravenes the Mosaic Law in the antitheses of 5:21-48, and other places in the Gospels. For example, in Matthew 12, Jesus reinterprets the Sabbath command (see verses 6, 8, 12), and Mark's interpretive comment makes this crystal clear that Jesus had annulled

---

Gaebelein (Grand Rapids, MI: Zondervan, 1995), 140-62; Vern S. Poythress, *The Shadow of Christ in the Law of Moses* (Phillipsburg, NJ: P & R Publishing, 1991), 251-86.

[81] Moo, "Jesus and the Mosaic Law," 18.

[82] Contra Schreiner, *New Testament Theology*, 628.

[83] Carson writes, "It must be frankly admitted that here Jesus formally contravenes OT law: what it permits or commands (Deut 6:13), he forbids," in *Matthew*, 154; Also see Thielman, *The Theology of the New Testament*, 87-88; idem, *The Law and the NT*, 49-58; Moo, "Jesus and the Mosaic Law," 17; idem, "The Law of Moses or the Law of Christ," in Feinberg, *Continuity and Discontinuity*, 204-05; John G. Reisinger, *But I Say Unto You* (Frederick, MD: New Covenant Media, 2006); Craig L. Blomberg, *Matthew*, in vol. 22 of *The New American Commentary*, ed. David S. Dockery (Nashville: Broadman Press, 1992), 103-05.

the Levitical food laws: "Thus he declared all foods clean" (7:19). In his teaching on divorce, Jesus shows that the created order trumps the Mosaic order (Matt 19:3-11). The answer to how Jesus does not abolish the Law and the Prophets becomes clear when we rightly define "fulfill." In light of the above (all too brief) considerations, it should be taken to mean that Jesus fulfills the Law and the Prophets "in that they point to him, and he is their fulfillment."[84] He brings that to pass which the Law and Prophets pointed to, and in this way, fulfills them. This interpretation fits with Matthew 11:13, where Matthew writes, "For all the Prophets and the Law prophesied until John" (cf. Luke 16:16-17, Matt 17:1-8, Rom 3:21).[85] D.A. Carson writes, "The entire Old Testament has a prophetic function; and Jesus came to fulfill the Old Testament."[86] It

---

[84] Carson, *Matthew,* 143; So also Thielman, *Theology of the New Testament,* 88; Poythress, *The Shadow of Christ,* 265; Moo, "Jesus and the Mosaic Law," 24-25; idem, "The Law of Moses or the Law of Christ," 205; Tom Wells and Fred Zaspel, *New Covenant Theology* (Frederick, MD: New Covenant Media, 2002), 109-22.

[85] See D.A. Carson, "Do the Prophets and the Law Quit Prophesying Before John? A Note on Matthew 11:13," in *The Gospels and the Scriptures of Israel,* ed. Craig A. Evans and W. Richard Stegner (England: Sheffield Academic Press, 1994), 179-94.

[86] D.A Carson, *The Sermon on the Mount: An Evangelical Exposition of Matthew 5-7* (Grand Rapids, MI: Baker Book House, 1978), 36. Thielman similarly writes, "The Mosaic Law was incomplete as it stood, and Jesus brought it to its eschatological fulfillment," in *Theology of the New Testament,* 88.

is in this sense that not a "dot" or an "iota"[87] will pass
away from the Law until all is accomplished (v. 18),[88] but
it must always be interpreted in light of the coming of
Christ.[89] Thomas Schreiner writes, "Jesus likely means
that the OT law continues to be authoritative for believers,
but only insofar as it is fulfilled in Jesus Christ. Such a fulfillment means that there are elements of continuity and
discontinuity. Moreover, the subsequent verses (Matt.
5:21-48) reveal that Jesus is the sovereign interpreter of
the law,"[90] The locus of authority for the new covenant
community no longer lies in Moses or the Prophets but in

---

[87] These terms are all-embracive. Hence, the tripartite division
of the Law is fundamentally flawed. See D.A Carson, *Sermon
on the Mount*, 35-36; Femi Adeyemi, "The New Covenant
and the Law of Christ," *Bibliotheca Sacra* 163.652, (October-
December 2006), 445-46; David A. Dorsey, "The Law of
Moses and the Christian: A Compromise," *The Journal of the
Evangelical Theological Society* 34.3, (September 1991), 329-
332.

[88] Don Garlington argues that the phrase "until heaven and
earth pass away" (5:18) is apocalyptic metaphor to say that
the Law "remains intact until such time as the new creation
comes." Since the time of the Law and Prophets ceases with
Christ, who inaugurates the new creation epoch, the Law
passes from the scene, in "Oath-Taking in the Community of
the New Age," *Trinity Journal* 16, no. 2 (Fall 1995): 154-56.
This view deserves serious consideration (but cf. Luke 16:16-
17).

[89] Moo, "The Law of Moses or the Law of Christ," 218; idem,
"Jesus and the Mosaic Law," 30.

[90] Schreiner, New Testament Theology, 628.

Jesus Christ, the "climax of the Old Testament's covenantal promises."[91]

In Luke 22:20, while instituting the Lord's Supper, Jesus says, "This cup that is poured out for you is the new covenant in my blood." Matthew's Gospel adds "which is poured out for many for the forgiveness of sins" (26:28), alluding to the suffering servant of Isaiah 53 (Isa 42:6, 53:10-12). The phrases "new covenant" (*kainē diathēkē*) and "forgiveness of sins" clearly recall Jeremiah's prophecy in chapter 31.[92] Mark's use of "blood of the covenant" alludes to Exodus 24:8 (cf. Zech 9:11) where Moses sprinkled blood on the people at the establishment of the Mosaic Covenant.[93] Jesus instituted a new Passover in part because he understood the violent and bloody death he was about to undergo as a new exodus (Isa 11:16, Luke

---

[91] Williamson, *Sealed with an Oath*, 184. Carson writes, "The Law and the Prophets point toward him, but he himself determines their meaning, fulfillment, and continuity, with an authority nothing less than divine," in *Sermon on the Mount*, 54. Also see Tom Wells, *The Priority of Jesus Christ* (Frederick, MD: New Covenant Media, 2005).

[92] Herman Ridderbos, *The Coming of the Kingdom* (Philadelphia: The Presbyterian and Reformed Publishing Co, 1962), 200-01.

[93] David W. Pao and Eckhard J. Schnabel, "Luke," in *Commentary on the New Testament Use of the Old Testament*, ed. G.K. Beale and D.A. Carson (Grand Rapids, MI: Baker Academic, 2007), 381-83; Also Frank Thielman, *Paul & The Law: A Contextual Approach* (Downers Grove, IL: InterVarsity Press, 1994), 105.

9:31), and the sacrificial rite by which the new covenant would be solemnly ratified.

THE WRITINGS OF PAUL

N.T. Wright says, "Covenant theology is one of the main clues, usually neglected, for understanding Paul."[94] Second Corinthians 3:4-4:18 is an important text on the relation of the old and new covenants in Paul. He expounds the superiority of the ministry of the new covenant over the old.[95] He writes that God "made us competent to be ministers of a new covenant, not of the letter but of the Spirit. For the letter (*gramma*) kills, but the Spirit (*pneuma*) gives life (3:6, cf. Rom 2:29, 7:6). The context makes clear that Paul uses "letter" to refer to the Mosaic Law (3:3), which has an inseparable connection to the Mosaic Covenant in 2 Corinthians 3.[96] The *gramma/pneuma* contrast should be understood in terms of salvation history.[97] Paul continues, agreeing that the old covenant came

---

[94] Wright, *Climax of the Covenant,* xi. Wright is *not* referring to the theological system of Reformed Covenant Theology. It should also be noted that this author does not endorse N.T. Wright's views concerning the new perspective on Paul.

[95] For a treatment of Exodus 32-34 as the backdrop for 2 Corinthians 3:7-18, see Hafemann, *2 Corinthians,* 142-44.

[96] Thomas R. Schreiner lists six reasons for seeing letter as the Mosaic law, in *The Law and Its Fulfillment: A Pauline Theology of Law* (Grand Rapids, MI: Baker Books, 1993), 81-82, also cf. 129. Also see Thielman, *Paul and the Law,* 111.

[97] Thomas R. Schreiner, *Paul: Apostle of God's Glory* (Downers Grove, IL: IVP Academic, 2001), 134-35; idem, *New Testament Theology,* 480-81; Hafemann, *2 Corinthians,* 131.

with glory, but the new covenant ministry of the Spirit has even more (3:7-8, cf. John 1:16)! Verses 9-11 are crystal clear: "For if there was glory in the ministry of condemnation, the ministry of righteousness must far exceed it in glory. Indeed, in this case, what once had glory has come to have no glory at all, because of the glory that surpasses it. For if what was being brought to an end came with glory, much more will what is permanent have glory." Paul is saying that there was nothing inherently wrong with the old covenant, but it has served its purpose in salvation history, and is now being brought to an end (3:13: *eis to telos*[98] *tou katargoumenou*). Wright similarly notes, "The Torah is given for a specific period of time, and is then set aside—not because it was a bad thing now happily abolished, but because it was a good thing whose purpose has now been accomplished. [The old covenant] was

---

[98] Schreiner writes, "What is particularly instructive is that in every other passage in the New Testament where a preposition occurs before [telos], it never means 'goal' or 'outcome' or 'result.' In fact, in seven of these thirteen texts the temporal meaning is clearly present. The temporal meaning is quite possibly present in four other texts with a prepositional phrase, and once again the meaning 'goal' or 'outcome' is not possible in these texts. The prepositional phrase . . . . (eis to telos) in 2 Corinthians 3:13, therefore, probably means 'to the end.' And even if [telos] does mean 'goal,' the idea of cessation of the law is still found in the verb pass away," in *Law and Its Fulfillment*, 133.

always *intended* to be a temporary mode of administration."[99]

The problem was not so much with the covenant as with the covenant community. The "era of letter" was inferior due to the lack of the Spirit.[100] The old covenant community had no power to obey, so without the Spirit, the letter kills.[101] The pouring out of the Spirit, which has its basis in Christ's cross-work, constitutes an eschatological advance on the old covenant.[102] Paul concludes the chapter explaining that the hearts of the Israelites were veiled, because they have not been given a heart to understand or eyes to see or ears to hear (Deut 29:4), but Christ, who is the Spirit (3:17-18), brings freedom when one turns to the Lord. Christ brings the internalization of the law (Jer 31:31-34), the distribution of the Spirit (Joel 2, Acts 2), replaces stony hearts with hearts of flesh (Ezek 11:19, 36:26), and illumines minds to see the true purpose of the

---

[99] Wright, Climax of the Covenant, 181, cf. 266. So also Schriener, Law and Its Fulfillment, 132; Williamson, Sealed with an Oath, 193.

[100] Hence, elsewhere Paul uses the phrase "under law" to refer to the old age of redemptive history when the Mosaic Covenant was still operative. Under law is equivalent to being under sin (see Gal 5:18, Rom 6:14-15). Also see Schreiner, *New Testament Theology*, 534, 647-48; Moo, "The Law of Moses or the Law of Christ," 210-15.

[101] Schreiner, *Law and Its Fulfillment*, 82-83, 130; Hafemann, *2 Corinthians*, 132.

[102] Note the contrasts in verse 7-11: Now if … even more glory (7-8), For if … must far exceed it in glory (9), For if … much more (11). See Thielman, *Paul and Law*, 112-13.

Torah. So from this passage we see the newness and superiority of the new covenant against the inferior old covenant which is passing away having served its purpose.

First Corinthians 7:19 is also an informative passage on Paul's view of the law-covenant. He writes, "For neither circumcision counts for anything nor uncircumcision, but keeping the commandments of God." For those familiar with the old covenant, this statement would seem to be a contradiction. For the Jew, not only did circumcision count, it counted for everything![103] D.A. Carson aptly writes, "The average first-century Jew would have said, 'Wait a minute! Circumcision *is* one of God's commands. How can you say that circumcision is nothing, and then immediately comment, 'Keeping God's commands is what counts'?' The only answer is that, for Paul, the commands of God that he finds operative for the Christian cannot be equated with the Mosaic Code."[104] Those united to Christ by faith no longer look to Moses, the me-

---

[103] Gordon D. Fee, *The Epistle to the Corinthians* in *The New International Commentary on the New Testament,* ed. Gordon Fee (Grand Rapids, MI: Eerdmans, 1987), 313. Thielman shows when Jesus answers the rich young ruler in Matthew 19, he says "keep the commandments" (*tērēson tas entolas*), then lists commandments from Lev 19:18. Also, the LXX translation of Ezra 9:4 uses "the commandments of God" as a synonym for the Law of Moses. "The phrase Paul has chosen to refer to God's commandments, therefore, is one that in his cultural context clearly referred to the Mosaic Law," in *Paul and the Law,* 101.

[104] D.A Carson, *The Cross and Christian Ministry* (Grand Rapids, MI: Baker Books, 1993), 119.

diator of the old covenant, but to their rightful Lord Jesus Christ, the mediator of a new and better covenant.

First Corinthians 9:20b-21 is another case in point. Paul writes, "To those under the law I became as one under the law (though not being myself under the law) that I might win those under the law. To those outside the law I became as one outside the law (not being outside the law of God but under the law of Christ) that I might win those outside the law." Paul is clear here that he is *not* "under law" (*hupo nomon*), and is not "without the law of God" (*mē ōn anomos theou*), but "under the law of Christ" or literally "in-lawed to Christ" (*ennomos Christou*). Paul is not under the Mosaic law-covenant like the Jews, but can become as one who is under law-covenant; nor is he without the law (*anamois*) like the Gentiles, but can become as the Gentiles who are without the law. But Paul is no antinomian! He is not outside the law of God, but under the law of Christ! Again, Carson writes, "Apparently, then, Paul sees himself in a *tertium quid*: he neither sees himself under the law-covenant, nor does he see himself as completely lawless. ... Rather, he thinks of himself in a third position, a distinctly Christian position, needing to flex one way in the evangelization of Jews, and needing to flex another way in the evangelization of Gentiles."[105] It can be

---

[105] D.A. Carson, "Mystery and Fulfillment: Toward a More Comprehensive Paradigm of Paul's Understanding of the Old and the New," in D.A. Carson (ed.), *Justification and Variegated Nomism, Volume 2: The Paradoxes of Paul* (Tubingen: Mohr Siebeck; Grand Rapids: Baker Academic, 2004), 402-03; idem, *Cross and Christian Ministry*, 118. C.H. Dodd similarly summarizes the debate: "Paul declares that he is not

safely said that Paul equates the law of God with the law of Christ, which is equivalent to the "commandments of God" in 7:19, which are all distinct from the Mosaic Law.[106] Christians, no longer subject to the temporary Mosaic law-covenant, are subject to the jurisdiction of Jesus, mediator of the new covenant.[107]

Although not explicitly dealing with the new covenant, Galatians 3:15-4:7 is a very important passage for understanding Paul's "covenantal theology."[108] In this section, as with 2 Corinthians 3 above, when Paul uses "law" (*ho nomos*), he is referring to the Mosaic law-covenant.[109] Paul

---

[*hupo nomon*], meaning, not subject to Torah. His Jewish adversary counters, 'Then you are, by your own confession, [*anomos*], a lawless, ungovernable, dissolute heathen.' 'No,' Paul retorts, 'you are assuming an unwarranted identity of the Torah with the ultimate law of God. A man may be free from Torah and yet be loyal to the law of God, as it is represented or expressed in the law of Christ. Being myself subject to the law of Christ, I am no stranger to the law of God, although I claim freedom from the Torah,'" in *More New Testament Studies* (Grand Rapids, MI: Eerdmans, 1968), 136.

[106] Thielman, Paul and the Law, 104.

[107] Adeyemi, "The New Covenant Law and the Law of Christ," 441; Carson, *Cross and Christian Ministry,* 120; Wells, *The Priority of Jesus Christ.*

[108] Wright, Climax of the Covenant, 156.

[109] So Linda L. Belleville, "'Under Law': Structural Analysis and the Pauline Concept of Law in Galatians 3.21-4.11," *Journal for the Study of the New Testament* 26 (1986): 71; John H. Walton, *Covenant: God's Purpose God's Plan* (Grand Rapids, MI:

wrote to counter the Judaizers who, along with many Jews, viewed the Mosaic Covenant as God's final revelation to his people, and considered it supreme in his dealings with them as well.[110] They viewed the law as an eternal end in itself, and in so doing "committed a serious time-keeping blunder."[111] The apostle begins his argument by showing that the promises were made to Abraham and his offspring, not offsprings referring to many, but referring to one, who is Christ (3:16). Then Paul reads the Bible sequentially to show that the promise was given to Abraham 430 years prior to the giving of the law (3:17). The inheritance comes by promise, not law, for the promise was given before the law. Paul is saying, in essence, "Any good Bible reader should see the superiority of the Abrahamic covenant." His hermeneutic is grounded in salvation history, not "how much space is given over to the law in the sacred text, or how large a role it played in the history of Israel."[112]

Zondervan, 1994), 166; Schreiner, *Law and Its Fulfillment,* 33-40, 126; idem, "The Commands of God," 68, 77; Dumbrell, *The End of the Beginning,* 113; Thielman, *Paul and the Law,* 108.

[110] Schreiner, *Law and Its Fulfillment,* 124-26. Also see Carson, "Mystery and Fulfillment," 411, who cites *Wis* 18:4, *Ag. Ap.* 2.277, *Mos* 2.14, *Jub* 1.27, 3:31, 6:17.

[111] Thielman, Theology of the New Testament, 266

[112] Carson, "Mystery and Fulfillment," 412. Carson also writes, "Even though relatively little space is devoted in the Old Testament to Adam or to the promises to Abraham, and far more space is devoted in the Old Testament to the law-covenant (not only in the Books of Moses but in the histori-

Paul, anticipating the question of the point in giving the law, answers that it was given "because of transgressions," that is, to reveal and even cause sin (3:19, cf. Rom 5:20, 7, 2 Cor 3:6).[113] But the law is not contrary to the promises of God, "for if a law had been given that could give life, then righteousness would indeed be by the law" (3:21). Verses 23-26 are very important in Paul's argument:

> "Now before faith came, we were held captive under the law, imprisoned until the coming faith would be revealed. So then, the law was our guardian until Christ came, in order that we might be justified by faith. But now that faith has come, we are no longer under a guardian, for in Christ Jesus you are all sons of God, through faith."

The word that Paul uses for "guardian" (paidagōgos) is important in the structure of Paul's argument. Paul was not using the term in an educational sense, despite our

---

cal narratives that describe the history of Israel as a nation and in the prophetic words that call Israel back to that covenant), once the importance of the story-line is grasped, then determining what is of most controlling importance cannot be discovered by measuring what themes take up the most space. In other words, Paul assesses the significance of Israel and the Sinai covenant *within the larger biblical narrative*," 427.

113 Schreiner, *Law and Its Fulfillment*, 74-77; Thielman, *Paul and the Law*, 132; Ridderbos, *Paul, 150*, who notes, "This is the awful sharpness of the antithesis between Paul's doctrine of the law and that of the synagogue," 151.

use of the derivative "pedagogue."[114] In ancient Greco-Roman society, the *paidagōgos* was a domestic slave within the household who was responsible for supervising the children from infancy to late adolescence.[115] *Paidagōgos* is probably best translated "babysitter"[116] in this context, as Paul clearly uses the term to refer to the law-covenant's temporal nature.[117] Guardians were only needed until maturity was reached, then they became unnecessary.

Galatians 3-4 is a salvation-historical argument (cf. also Rom 4:1-12 and Heb 3:7-4:13, 7) showing that the Mosaic law-covenant was intended to be an "interim covenant." While the Jew treated the law as eternal, Paul relativizes it as a parenthesis in redemptive history.[118] The law was our

---

[114] Richard N. Longenecker writes, "For while today we think of pedagogues as teachers, in antiquity a *paidagōgos* was distinguished from a *didaskalos* ('teacher') and had custodial and disciplinary functions rather than educative or instructional ones," in *Galatians*, in *Word Biblical Commentary*, vol. 41, ed. Ralph P. Martin (Columbia: Nelson Reference & Electronic, 1990), 146. So also Moo, "The Law of Moses or the Law of Christ," 214.

[115] See Belleville, "'Under Law'," 59; Thielman, *Paul and the Law*, 132; Longenecker, *Galatians*, 148.

[116] Schreiner, *New Testament Theology*, 366, 534, 646; idem, "The Commands of God," 83.

[117] Moo, "The Law of Moses or the Law of Christ," 214; Thielman, *Paul and the Law*, 133; Schreiner, *Paul*, 128-30; idem, *Law and Its Fulfillment*, 78-80.

[118] Wright, *Climax of the Covenant*, 266; So also William J. Dumbrell, "Abraham and the Abrahamic covenant in Galatians 3:1-14," in *The Gospel to the Nations: Perspectives on Paul's Mission*, ed. Peter Bolt and Mark Thompson (Downers

guardian *until* Christ came (3:24, cf. 3:19, 3:23). The child, utterly lacking freedom,[119] is under guardians and managers *until* the date set by his father (4:2). Schreiner writes, "Paul reasons here that the Mosaic covenant was designed to be in force for a certain period of salvation history, as an interim measure until the promise given to Abraham was fulfilled. With the coming of Christ the role of the Mosaic covenant has ceased. Believers are no longer under the pedagogue of the law."[120]

Paul rounds out his argument showing that all who exercise faith in Jesus Christ are Abraham's offspring. Believers in Christ share in the inheritance by union with Christ, whether Jew or Gentile, slave or free, or male or female. Before Christ came, the children were under guardians and managers, enslaved to the elementary principles of the world,[121] but now that the fullness of

---

Grove, IL: InterVarsity Press, 2000), 22; idem, *Search for Order*, 293; Carson, "Mystery and Fulfillment," 412; Schriener, *Law and Its Fulfillment*, 123-43; Thielman, *Paul and the Law*, 131.

[119] Herman Ridderbos, *Paul: An Outline of His Theology* (Grand Rapids, MI: Eerdmans, 1966), 148; Belleville, "'Under Law'," 60; Longenecker, *Galatians*, 148;

[120] Schreiner, Law and Its Fulfillment, 128.

[121] Clinton E. Arnold convincingly argues that the "principles of the world (*stoicheia*) should be interpreted as demonic powers equivalent to the principalities and powers, in "Returning to the Domain of the Powers: *Stoicheia* as Evil Spirits in Galatians 4:3, 9," *Novum Testamentum* 38.1 (January 1996): 55-76; idem, *Powers of Darkness: Principalities and Powers in*

time has come, "God sent forth his Son, born of woman, born under the law, to redeem those who were under the law, so that we might receive adoption as sons. Being sons rather than slaves, God has also given us the Spirit of his Son and making us an heir through God (4:1-7). The Galatians have begun to experience the fulfillment of the Abrahamic promise with the receiving of the Spirit, and have been delivered from the present evil age (1:4), but as Frank Thielman writes, they "have started a futile attempt to swim against the current of salvation history,"[122] preferring the bridled life of a minor by "turning back to the weak and worthless elementary principles of the world" (4:9, cf. 4:3, note 121). The Abrahamic covenant is foundational, for it was given long before Moses was even on the scene, but it is foundational only in that it points to the true seed and faithful new covenant mediator,[123] Jesus

---

Paul's Letters (Downers Grove, IL: InterVarsity Press, 1992), 53, 131-32.

[122] Thielman, Theology of the New Testament, 268.

[123] See R. Fowler White, "The Last Adam and His Seed: An Exercise in Theological Preemption," *Trinity Journal* 6, no. 1 (Spring 1985): 60-73 for an excellent treatment of the genealogical principle in the new covenant. All of Christ's "seed" by definition have the Spirit. Before Christ, the relationships between the covenant family and the covenant head were defined in physical terms. Williamson writes, "While certainly including biological descendants of Abraham, this new covenant community is not defined by biological ancestry but rather by spiritual descent," in *Sealed with an Oath*, 146.

Christ, who is both the goal and end (*telos*) of the law (Rom 10:4, cf. 2 Cor 3:11,13).[124]

HEBREWS

The book of Hebrews may be the clearest teaching on the newness of the new covenant, perhaps being "the most Christ-centered of all the Epistles."[125] Its teaching makes clear that Jesus' death on the cross was the foundational sacrificial rite by which the new covenant is inaugurated, its provisions are activated, and the old covenant is superseded.[126] Our focus will be on chapters 7-9, but a short summary for the book of Hebrews could be: "Jesus is better." The epistle begins, "Long ago, at many times and in many ways, God spoke to our fathers by the prophets, but in these last days he has spoken to us by his Son" (1:1). Here we already have a hint of contrast be-

---

[124] On Rom 10:4, see Moo, "The Law of Moses or the Law of Christ," 206-208; Blaising and Bock, *Progressive Dispensationalism*, 195-96; Schreiner, *Paul*, 122; idem, *New Testament Theology*, 577, 649.

[125] Richard D. Phillips, *Hebrews*, in *Reformed Expository Commentary*, ed. Richard D. Phillips and Philip Graham Ryken (Phillipsburg, NJ: P&R Publishing, 2006), 624. Phillips also writes, "One of the main purposes of the Book of Hebrews is to bring the old covenant in Moses and the new covenant in Christ into proper relationship," 231. So also Williamson: "The most developed 'new covenant theology' in the New Testament is found in Hebrews," in *Sealed with an Oath*, 201.

[126] Williamson, *Sealed with an Oath*, 192, 194, 200; Blaising and Bock, *Progressive Dispensationalism*, 202.

tween Jesus and Moses in the first verse of Hebrews since Moses was considered the greatest of the prophets, who are inferior to the Son, through whom God has spoken with finality (1:1). It is not by accident that Hebrews begins by demonstrating the superiority of Jesus over the angels (1:5-14). It was broadly accepted among the Jews that the law of God had been mediated to Moses and delivered to Israel through angels (see Heb 2:2, Deut 33:2, Acts 7:38, 53, Gal 3:19).[127] The new revelation given in the Son is superior to the old revelation given by the prophets and through the mediation of angels. Then Hebrews presents Christ as the true human (Ps 8, Gen 1:26-28) who restores our humanity by tasting death for everyone and destroying the devil (2:5-18).[128] Next, Jesus, the *Son* who is faithful *over* God's house, is presented as greater than Moses, a faithful *servant in* God's house (3:1-6). Jesus is also greater than Joshua (3:7-4:13). Joshua led the people into the land (Josh 21:43-45), but much later David wrote, "Today, if you hear his voice, do not harden your hearts" (3:7 quoting Ps 95). An eschatological Sabbath rest still awaited the people of God and Jesus, the Lord of the Sab-

---

[127] William L. Lane, *Hebrews: A Call to Commitment* (Vancouver: Regent College Publishing, 1985), 20, 34, 39, 57; Phillips, *Hebrews*, 27; Thielman, *Law and the New Testament*, 113.

[128] I am indebted to Stephen J. Wellum, "Issues in Biblical and Systematic Theology Handouts" (classroom lecture notes, 27077—*Issues in Biblical and Systematic Theology*, Summer 2008, photocopy), and D.A. Carson, "Hard Texts: Why Does Hebrews Cite the Old Testament Like That 1-3," (lectures held for the J.B. Gay Lectures at The Southern Baptist Theological Seminary, Louisville, KY, 28 February 2005) for their exegetical insight regarding the book of Hebrews.

bath (Matt 12), has brought Sabbath rest for those who trust him *today* (Matt 11:28-30). The author begins to show how Jesus fulfills the Levitical priesthood (5:1-10), but pauses to warn the people of the dangers of not persevering.

Hebrews picks back up the teaching concerning Christ's priesthood in chapter 7. He begins by making a few exegetical comments on Genesis 14:17-20, and then shows how Melchizedek, priestly-king of (Jeru)Salem blessed Abraham and received a tithe from him, making Melchizedek superior. Melchizedek also lacks a genealogy, which is a very significant literary observation in the text of Genesis.[129] Since Levi was not even born yet, he in some sense paid tithes to Melchizedek, again showing the superiority of the Melchizedekian priestly order that has no end. Verses 11-12 are a key transition point: "Now if perfection had been attainable through the Levitical priesthood (for under it the people received the law), what further need would there have been for another priest to arise after the order of Melchizedek, rather than one named after the order of Aaron? For when there is a change in the priesthood, there is necessarily a change in the law as well." There are two main points to note from this passage. First, the old covenant must be seen as a package. It is a whole unit, consisting of law, covenant, and priesthood.[130] Second, God never intended for the old

---

[129] See Genesis 2:4, 5:1, 6:9, 10:1, 11:10, 11:27, 25:12, 25:19, 36:1, 36:9, 37:2.

[130] Those who attempt to make a tripartite distinction within the law must avoid this passage to do so. One cannot divorce a

covenant to bring ultimate salvation (perfection). This is why David, hundreds of years after Genesis 14, wrote of a new priestly order to come: "You are a priest forever, after the order of Melchizedek" (Heb 7:17 quoting Ps 110). The "former commandment is set aside because of its weakness and uselessness (for the law made nothing perfect)" (7:18-19). But now Christ has arrived, the true and faithful high priest who became a priest, "not on the basis of a legal requirement concerning bodily descent, but by the power of an indestructible life" (7:16). He holds his priesthood permanently, and is therefore able "to save to the uttermost those who draw near to God through him" (7:24-25). Christ has no need to sacrifice for his sin and the sins of the people again and again because "he did this once for all when he offered up himself" (7:27).

Since the law-covenant was a package deal, Christ not only brings a new priesthood, but is also "guarantor of a better covenant" (7:22).[131] Chapter 8 develops this argument and verses 6-13 are worth quoting at length:

---

covenant from its stipulations. The law is contained within the covenant. So Schreiner, "The Commands of God," 68, 77; Dumbrell, *End from the Beginning*, 113; Adeyemi, "The New Covenant Law," 446; idem, "What is the New Covenant," 320; Thielman, *Law and the New Testament*, 111, 131. Barry C. Joslin argues that "law" and "covenant" are very closely related, but not synonyms, in "The Theology of the Mosaic Law in Hebrews 7:1-10:18" (Ph.D. diss., The Southern Baptist Theological Seminary, 2005), 200-06.

[131] Frank Thielman lists three reasons why the new covenant is better: It is immutable and eternal, this promise came after the law in time, taking precedence over it, and the affiliation of the promise with God's eternally perfected Son rather

But as it is, Christ has obtained a ministry that is as much more excellent than the old as the covenant he mediates is better, since it is enacted on better promises. For if that first covenant had been faultless, there would have been no occasion to look for a second. For he finds fault with them when he says: "Behold, the days are coming, declares the Lord, when I will establish a new covenant with the house of Israel and with the house of Judah, not like the covenant that I made with their fathers on the day when I took them by the hand to bring them out of the land of Egypt. For they did not continue in my covenant, and so I showed no concern for them, declares the Lord. For this is the covenant that I will make with the house of Israel after those days, declares the Lord: I will put my laws into their minds, and write them on their hearts, and I will be their God, and they shall be my people. And they shall not teach, each one his neighbor and each one his brother, saying, 'Know the Lord,' for they shall all know me, from the least of them to the greatest. For I will be merciful toward their iniquities, and I will remember their sins no more." In speaking of a new covenant, he makes the first one obsolete. And what is becoming obsolete and growing old is ready to vanish away.

In these verses we have the longest quotation of the OT in the NT with Hebrews quoting Jeremiah 31:31-34. We have already laid out the details of this passage above, so here the comments will be brief. Again, like the Apostle Paul, the author of Hebrews is simply reading his Old Testa-

---

than with sinful and weak priests demonstrates the superiority of this covenant to the Mosaic law, in *Law and the New Testament*, 122.

ment chronologically.[132] If the old covenant was God's eternal and immutable plan for his people, there would have never been a new covenant promised. The author understands the rich Jeremiah passage as a direct verbal prophecy, fulfilled by the inauguration of the new covenant in Christ's sacrificial death and triumphant exaltation to service as a better high priest.[133] Hebrews agrees with Paul[134] and Jesus that the old covenant was intended to be an interim covenant, merely a shadow (*skia*) of the good things to come instead of the true form of these realities (Heb 10:1, cf. Col 2:17). The argument of Hebrews is that the Jew should have understood the self-confessed inadequacy of the old order (Ps 8, 95, 110, Jer 31).[135] The problem was the people, who did not continue in the covenant (8:9). The old covenant "had proved ineffective to

---

[132] Carson, "Evangelicals, Ecumenism, & the Church," 361; idem, "Mystery and Fulfillment," 428 n.99.

[133] George H. Guthrie, "Hebrews," in *Commentary on the NT Use of the OT*, ed. Beale and Carson, 972.

[134] Concerning Paul and the author of Hebrews, Thielman writes, "The sweeping nature of the argument in each case makes it impossible to claim that the two authors describe the obsolescence of only certain parts of the Mosaic law or merely criticize the law's misuse: the entire Mosaic dispensation has reached its divinely appointed end," in *The Law and the New Testament*, 177; F.F. Bruce, *The Epistle to the Hebrews*, in *The New International Commentary on the New Testament*, ed. Gordon Fee (Grand Rapids, MI: Eerdmans, 1990), 166-67.

[135] George B. Caird, "The Exegetical Method of Hebrews," *Canadian Journal of Theology* 5 (1959): 44-51.

create a faithful people,"[136] not supplying the power of the Spirit or full and final forgiveness of sins. Since the new covenant has been ratified by the sacrificial death of the new Melchizedekian priest, the old covenant has been made obsolete (8:13). The language could not be any clearer.[137] The new covenant will be an unbreakable and effective covenant producing a community in which every last member knows the Lord, has the Spirit, and is fully forgiven in Christ. As glorious as the inaugurated new covenant blessings that Christians now experience are, we still await the final reality that the new covenant points to: eternal life in the presence of God on a new earth (Isa 65:17, Rev 21-22).[138]

---

[136] George Eldon Ladd, *A Theology of the New Testament* (Grand Rapids, MI: Eerdmans, 1993), 629.

[137] Those who argue for a "renewed" covenant rather than a new are imposing a theological grid onto the text of Scripture. Jer 31 and Heb 8 are clearly referring to a new covenant that is not like the old, and indeed, supersedes the old. Contra Phillips, *Hebrews*, 234. See Adeyemi, "What is the New Covenant 'Law' in Jeremiah 31:33?," 318-21; Williamson, *Sealed with an Oath*, 202.

[138] Williamson, Sealed with an Oath, 208-10; Dumbrell, End of the Beginning, 94-95.

CHAPTER 4
CONCLUSION

The relationship between the Testaments is a very controversial matter with massive implications for Christian theology and practice.[139] Richard Lints goes so far as to say, "I suspect that almost all major controversies in evangelical theology could be reduced in the end to a difference concerning the relationship of the Testaments."[140] This book has argued on the basis of the progressive covenantal outlook of the OT, and several key passages in the NT from different authors, that the new covenant is radically and eschatologically *new*. Canonically-informed exegesis shows the impossibility of viewing the new covenant as simply a "renewed" old covenant (see note 56 and 137). There are many covenants (Eph 2:12 – *diathēkōn*) within the one purpose of God (Eph 1:11, 3:11) and they all culminate in the new covenant. If the above exegesis is correct, the Reformed system of Covenant Theology with one overarching covenant of grace fails to do justice to the biblical Text by flattening out the covenants. Although having similarities to both Covenant Theology and Progressive Dispensationalism, the outlook of this book falls into a third system, namely, "New Covenant Theolo-

---

[139] E.g. ethics, law, ordinances, community, church discipline, and mission, to name a few.

[140] Richard Lints, *The Fabric of Theology: A prolegomenon to Evangelical Theology* (Grand Rapids, MI: Eerdmans, 1993), 301 n.13.

gy."[141] This outlook has significant implications for the nature of the church. The new covenant initiated by Christ's cross-work brings massive structural changes to the new covenant community. Now, all have the Spirit and know the Lord. In other words, the new covenant community, by definition, is a *believing* community. This third system of New Covenant Theology is needed in particular

---

[141] New Covenant Theology is often accused of being antinomian due to its denial of the Decalogue as the eternal moral law of God. This accusation is wrongheaded. As shown above, the new covenant believer is not without law, but under the law of Christ (Gal 6:2, 1 Cor 9:21). The moral demand of Christ goes beyond the moral demand of the old covenant, which makes the accusation all the more misplaced. On the law of Christ, see Moo, "The Law of Moses or the Law of Christ," 203-18; Thielman, *Law and the New Testament,* 33, 180; Schreiner, *New Testament Theology,* 621, 654; Reisinger, *But I Say Unto You;* Wells and Zaspel, *New Covenant Theology;* Dodd, *More New Testament Studies,* 147ff; Adeyemi, "What is the New Covenant 'Law' in Jeremiah 31:33?," 312-21; idem, "The New Covenant Law and the Law of Christ," 438-52; David Dorsey has a very helpful article on this issue, where he shows that the old covenant was made with a specific nation, is monolithic, the whole of it is "moral," and how that we as a new covenant people are unable to fulfill the vast majority of the old covenant stipulations. He argues that believers are not legally bound to any of the 613 commands of the old covenant, but all 613 commandments are binding upon Christians in a revelatory and pedagogical sense, in "The Law of Moses and the Christian: A Compromise," 321-34.

for a Baptist biblical theology.[142] More than any other system, New Covenant Theology does justice to the progressive nature of Scripture by seeking to let biblical theology inform systematic theology.

---

[142] The movement need not be monolithic, as today's Dispensationalism and Covenant Theology is far from monolithic. The basis for holding to New Covenant Theology could be as minimal as viewing: the new covenant community as all having the Spirit, Christ as the true Israel and the church inherits the promises by virtue of its union with Christ, the Mosaic covenant as an interim covenant, rejection of the Israel/church distinction, rejection of the tripartite distinction of the law, and the rejection of the theological category of the "covenant of grace."

BIBLIOGRAPHY

Adeyemi, Femi. "The New Covenant Law and the Law of Christ." *Bibliotheca Sacra* 163, no. 652 (October-December 2006): 438-52.

_____. "What Is The New Covenant "Law" In Jeremiah 31:33?" *Bibliotheca Sacra* 163, no. 651 (July-September 2006): 312-21.

Alexander, T.D. *From Paradise to the Promised Land.* Grand Rapids, MI: Baker Academic, 2002.

_____. "Genealogies, Seed and the Compositional Unity of Genesis." *Tyndale Bulletin* 44, no. 2 (November 1993): 255-70.

_____. "Royal Expectation in Genesis to Kings: The Importance of Biblical Theology." *Tyndale Bulletin* 49, no. 2 (November 1998): 191-212.

_____. "Seed." In *New Dictionary of Biblical Theology.* Edited by T. Desmond Alexander, et al. Downers Grove, IL: Inter-Varsity Press, 2000.

_____. *The Servant King.* Vancouver, British Columbia: Regent College Publishing, 1998.

Arnold, Clinton E. *Powers of Darkness: Principalities and Powers in Paul's Letters.* Downers Grove, IL: InterVarsity Press, 1992.

_____. "Returning to the Domain of the Powers: *Stoicheia* as Evil Spirits in Galatians 4:3, 9." *Novum Testamentum* 38, no. 1 (January 1996): 55-76.

Bartholomew, Craig G. "Covenant and Creation: Covenant Overload or Covenant Deconstruction." *Calvin Theological Journal* 30, no. 1 (April 1995): 11-33.

Beale, G. K. *The Temple and the Church's Mission: A Biblical Theology of the Dwelling Place of God.* Downers Grove, IL: InterVarsity Press, 2004.

Belleville, Linda L. "'Under Law': Structural Analysis and the Pauline Concept of Law in Galatians 3.21-4.11." *Journal for the Study of the New Testament* 26 (1986): 53-78.

Blaising, Craig A. and Darrell L. Bock. *Progressive Dispensationalism.* Grand Rapids, MI: Baker Books, 1993.

Blomberg, Craig L. *Matthew.* In vol. 22 of *The New American Commentary.* Edited by David S. Dockery. Nashville: Broadman Press, 1992.

Bruce, F.F. *The Epistle to the Hebrews.* In *The New International Commentary on the New Testament.* Edited by Gordon Fee. Grand Rapids, MI: Eerdmans, 1990.

Caird, George B. "The Exegetical Method of Hebrews." *Canadian Journal of Theology* 5 (1959): 44-51.

Carson, D.A. "Atonement in Romans 3:21-26." In *The Glory of the Atonement.* Edited by Charles E. Hill and Frank A. James III, 119-39. Downers Grove, IL: InterVarsity Press, 2004.

_____. "Hard Texts: Why Does Hebrews Cite the Old Testament Like That 1-3." Lectures presented for the J.B. Gay

Lectures at The Southern Baptist Theological Seminary, Louisville, KY, 28 February 2005.

_____. *The Cross and Christian Ministry*. Grand Rapids, MI: Baker Books, 1993.

_____. *The Gospel According to John*. In *The Pillar New Testament Commentary*. Edited by D.A. Carson. Grand Rapids, MI: Eerdmans, 1991.

_____. "Do the Prophets and the Law Quit Prophesying Before John? A Note on Matthew 11:13." In *The Gospels and the Scriptures of Israel*. Edited by Craig A. Evans and W. Richard Stegner, 179-94. England: Sheffield Academic Press, 1994.

_____. *The Sermon on the Mount: An Evangelical Exposition of Matthew 5-7*. Grand Rapids, MI: Baker Book House, 1978.

_____. *Christ & Culture Revisited*. Grand Rapids, MI: Eerdmans, 2008.

_____. "Evangelicals, Ecumenism and the Church." In *Evangelical Affirmations*. Edited by Kenneth S. Kantzer and Carl F.H. Henry, 347-85. Grand Rapids, MI: Academie Books, 1990.

_____. "Mystery and Fulfillment: Toward a More Comprehensive Paradigm of Paul's Understanding of the Old and the New." In *Justification and Variegated Nomism, Volume 2: The Paradoxes of Paul*, eds. D.A. Carson, Peter T. O'Brien, and Mark A. Seifrid, 393-436. Tubingen: Mohr Siebeck and Grand Rapids:Baker Academic, 2004.

_____. *Matthew*. Vol. 1. In *The Expositor's Bible Commentary*. Edited by Frank E. Gaebelein. Grand Rapids, MI: Zondervan, 1995.

_____. *Showing the Spirit: A Theological Exposition of 1 Corinthians 12-14*. Grand Rapids, MI: Baker Books, 1987.

Dempster, Stephen G. *Dominion and Dynasty: A Theology of the Hebrew Bible*. Downers Grove, IL: InterVarsity Press, 2003.

Dodd, C.H. *More New Testament Studies*. Grand Rapids, MI: Eerdmans, 1968.

Dorsey, David A. "The Law of Moses and the Christian: A Compromise." *Journal of the Evangelical Theological Society* 34, no. 3 (September 1991): 321-34.

Dumbrell, William J. "The Covenant with Abraham." *The Reformed Theological Review* 41, no. 2 (May-August 1982): 42-50.

_____. *The End of the Beginning: Revelation 21-22 and the Old Testament*. Eugene, OR: Wipf and Stock Publishers, 1985.

_____. "Abraham and the Abrahamic covenant in Galatians 3:1-14." In *The Gospel to the Nations: Perspectives on Paul's Mission*. Edited by Peter Bolt and Mark Thompston, 19-31. Downers Grove, IL: InterVarsity Press, 2000.

_____. *The Search for Order: Biblical Eschatology in Focus*. Eugene, OR: Wipf and Stock Publishers, 2001.

_____. *Covenant and Creation: A Theology of the Old Testament Covenants*. Carlisle: Paternoster Press, 1984.

Fee, Gordon D. *The Epistle to the Corinthians*. In *The New International Commentary on the New Testament*. Edited by Gordon Fee. Grand Rapids, MI: Eerdmans, 1987.

Feinberg, John S. *Continuity and Discontinuity: Perspectives on the Relationship Between the Old and New Testaments*. Wheaton, IL: Crossway Books, 1988.

Fesko, J. V. *Last Things First: Unlocking Genesis 1-3 with the Christ of Eschatology*. Scotland: Mentor, 2007.

Garlington, Don. "Oath-Taking in the Community of the New Age." *Trinity Journal* 16, no. 2 (Fall 1995): 139-70.

Gentry, Peter J. "Kingdom Through Covenant: Humanity as the Divine Image." *The Southern Baptist Journal of Theology* 12, no. 1 (Spring 2008): 16-42.

_____. "Rethinking the "Sure Mercies of David" in Isaiah 55:3." *Westminster Theological Journal* 69, no. 2 (Fall 2007): 279-304.

Guthrie, George H. "Hebrews." In *Commentary on the New Testament Use of the Old Testament*. Edited by G.K. Beale and D.A. Carson, 251-414. Grand Rapids, MI: Baker Academic, 2007.

Hafemann, Scott J. "The Covenant Relationship." In *Central Themes in Biblical Theology: Mapping Unity in Diversity*. Edited by Scott J. Hafemann and Paul R. House, 20-65. Grand Rapids: Baker Academic, 2007.

_____. *Second Corinthians*. In *The NIV Application Commentary*. Edited by Terry Muck. Grand Rapids, MI: Zondervan, 2000.

Hamilton, Jr., James M. *God's Indwelling Presence: The Holy Spirit in the Old and New Testaments.* Nashville, TN: B&H Academic, 2006.

Hoekema, Anthony A. *Created in God's Image.* Grand Rapids, MI: Eerdmans, 1986.

Horton, Michael. *God of Promise: Introducing Covenant Theology.* Grand Rapids, MI: Baker Books, 2006.

Joslin, Barry C. "The Theology of the Mosaic Law in Hebrews 7:1-10:18." Ph.D. diss., The Southern Baptist Theological Seminary, 2005.

Kaiser, Jr., Walter C. "The Blessing of David: The Charter of Humanity." In *The Law and the Prophets: Old Testament Studies Prepared in Honor of Oswald Thompson Allis.* Edited by John H. Skilton, 298-318. Nutley, NJ: Presbyterian and Reformed Publishing Co.. 1974.

Kostenberger, Andreas J. and Peter T. O'Brien. *Salvation to the Ends of the Earth: A Biblical Theology of Mission.* Downers Grove, IL: InterVarsity Press, 2001.

Ladd, George Eldon. *A Theology of the New Testament.* Grand Rapids, MI: Eerdmans, 1993.

Lane, William L. *Hebrews: A Call to Commitment.* Vancouver: Regent College Publishing, 1985.

Lints, Richard. *The Fabric of Theology: A prolegomenon to Evangelical Theology.* Grand Rapids, MI: Eerdmans, 1993.

Longenecker, Richard N. *Galatians.* In vol 41 of *Word Biblical Commentary.* Edited by Ralph P. Martin. Columbia: Nelson Reference & Electronic, 1990.

Meyer, Jason C. "Paul, the Mosaic Covenant, and Redemptive History." Ph.D. diss., The Southern Baptist Theological Seminary, 2007.

Moo, Douglas J. "The Law of Moses or the Law of Christ." In *Continuity and Discontinuity: Perspectives on the Relationship Between the Old and New Testaments*. Edited by John S. Feinberg, 203-18. Wheaton, IL: Crossway Books, 1988.

_____. "Jesus and the Authority of the Mosaic Law." *Journal for the Study of the New Testament* 20 (1984): 3-49.

_____. "Nature in the New Creations: New Testament Eschatology and the Environment." *Journal of the Evangelical Theological Society* 49, no. 3 (September 2006): 449-88.

Moule, C.F.D. *The Phenomenon of the New Testament*. London: SCM Press, 1967.

Niehaus, Jeffrey J. "An Argument Against Theologically Constructed Covenants." *Journal of the Evangelical Theological Society* 50, no. 2 (June 2007): 259-73.

_____. *God at Sinai*. Grand Rapids, MI: Zondervan, 1995.

Pao, David W. and Eckhard J. Schnabel. "Luke." In *Commentary on the New Testament Use of the Old Testament*. Edited by G.K. Beale and D.A. Carson, 251-414. Grand Rapids, MI: Baker Academic, 2007.

Phillips, Richard D. *Hebrews*. In *Reformed Expository Commentary*. Edited by Richard D. Phillips and Philip Graham Ryken. Phillipsburg, NJ: P&R Publishing, 2006.

Poythress, Vern S. *The Shadow of Christ in the Law of Moses*. Phillipsburg, NJ: P&R Publishing, 1991.

Reisinger, John G. *Abraham's Four Seeds: A Biblical Examination of the Presuppositions of Covenant Theology and Dispensationalism.* Frederick, MD: New Covenant Media, 1998.

_____. *But I Say Unto You.* Frederick, MD: New Covenant Media, 2006.

Ridderbos, Herman. *The Coming of the Kingdom.* Philadelphia: The Presbyterian and Reformed Publishing Co, 1962.

_____. *Paul: An Outline of His Theology.* Grand Rapids, MI: Eerdmans, 1966.

Schreiner, Thomas R. *The Law and Its Fulfillment: A Pauline Theology of Law.* Grand Rapids, MI: Baker Books, 1993.

_____. "The Commands of God." In *Central Themes in Biblical Theology: Mapping Unity in Diversity.* Edited by Scott J. Hafemann and Paul R. House, 66-101. Grand Rapids: Baker Academic, 2007.

_____. *New Testament Theology: Magnifying God in Christ.* Grand Rapids, MI: Baker Academic, 2008.

_____. *Paul: Apostle of God's Glory.* Downers Grove, IL: IVP Academic, 2001.

Thielman, Frank. *The Law and the New Testament: The Question of Continuity.* New York: The Crossroad Publishing Company, 1999.

_____. *Paul & the Law: A Contextual Approach.* Downers Grove, IL: InterVarsity Press, 1994.

_____. *Theology of the New Testament: A Canonical and Synthetic Approach.* Grand Rapids, MI: Zondervan, 2005.

Vickers, Brian. *Jesus' Blood and Righteousness: Paul's Theology of Imputation.* Wheaton, IL: Crossway Books, 2006.

Walton, John. *Covenant: God's Purpose God's Plan.* Grand Rapids, MI: Zondervan, 1994.

Wells, Tom and Fred Zaspel. *New Covenant Theology.* Frederick, MD: New Covenant Media, 2002.

Wells, Tom. *The Priority of Jesus Christ.* Frederick, MD: New Covenant Media, 2005.

Wellum, Stephen J. "Issues in Biblical and Systematic Theology Handouts." Classroom lecture notes, *27077—Issues in Biblical and Systematic Theology.*, Summer 2008. Photocopy.

_____. "Baptism and the Relationship Between the Covenants," In *Believers's Baptism: Sign of the New Covenant in Christ.* Edited by Thomas R. Schreiner and Shawn D. Wright, 97-161. Nashville, TN: B&H Academic, 2006.

White, A. Blake. "Christ as the Last Adam." *Adorare Mente* 1, no. 1 (Spring 2008): 30-42.

White, R. Fowler. "The Last Adam and His Seed: An Exercise in Theological Preemption." *Trinity Journal* 6, no. 1 (Spring 1985): 61-73.

Williams, Michael D. *Far As the Curse is Found.* Phillipsburg, NJ: P & R Publishing, 2005.

Williamson, Paul R. *Sealed with an Oath: Covenant in God's Unfolding Plan.* Downers Grove, IL: InterVarsity Press, 2007.

Wright, N.T. *The Climax of the Covenant.* Minneapolis: Fortress Press, 1993.

CPSIA information can be obtained
at www.ICGtesting.com
Printed in the USA
FSHW022004290421
80987FS